REMBRANDT

The World's Masters – New Series

by Anthony Bertram

THE STUDIO PUBLICATIONS LONDON & NEW YORK

FIRST PUBLISHED 1955

WORLD'S MASTERS NEW SERIES *Editor: ANTHONY BERTRAM*

The covers of this series, designed by Arthur Hundleby, are based on heraldic motives representing the national school to which each artist belongs or with which he is chiefly associated.

Already published

WILLIAM BLAKE

SANDRO BOTTICELLI

JAN VERMEER OF DELFT

HANS HOLBEIN THE YOUNGER

WILLIAM HOGARTH

JEAN AUGUSTE DOMINIQUE INGRES

PIERO DELLO FRANCESCA

EL GRECO

MICHELANGELO

PIETER BRUEGEL

EUGENIE DELACROIX

HIERONYMUS BOSCH

THE VAN EYCKS

MATHIAS GRÜNEWALD

PICASSO

GIOTTO

SICKERT

Others in preparation

Printed in Great Britain by William Clowes & Sons Ltd, London and Beccles. Published in London by the Studio Ltd, 66 Chandos Place, WC2 and in New York by the Studio Publications Inc, 432 Fourth Avenue

Introduction

WE can never disentangle what an artist owes to his own genius, in the sense of 'characteristic disposition', from what is inevitably to some extent imposed on him by the circumstances of his life. Since Dutch society in the seventeenth century was Protestant and mercantile, it did not demand altarpieces or church murals nor the sumptuous decoration of palaces, but small, comfortable and cheap pictures for middle-class homes. Moreover, the mercantile mind, having a great horror of the pig in a poke, was shy to commission. The artist generally painted first and sold afterwards, which meant that he had to keep his eye on the market. The only common exception to this was the portrait.

These circumstances certainly modified Rembrandt's art; but the essence of his genius, that which makes him one of the greatest European artists, was precisely that he reacted against and trans-cended the surrounding Dutchness. He was not simply the greatest among all those Dutchmen who painted with masterly skill and little vision: he was of a different kind. They were mostly—Vermeer is the outstanding exception—recorders of the pleasant, the amusing or the boisterous appearances of Dutch people and their behaviour and of the domestic beauties of Dutch towns and fields. But Rembrandt, peering into the shadows of the world's great hospital, revealed in a beam of light the significance of its saddest rags and bones.

What, then, was Dutch about him was his realism; what marked him off, what was of his private 'genius', was his vision of the poetry in human suffering. Like Wilfred Owen, he found that 'the poetry was in the pity'. But the poetry, of course, is also in the forms he created and inseparable from them, as Owen's poetry is inseparable from the actual words he wrote. But a visual poetry that is also pity will not produce something that is comfortable to live with, which the complacent particularly demand, as if a picture were a spiritual armchair. Therefore, Rembrandt did not treat his pictures as precious objects, to be smoothly and neatly 'finished'. (I am thinking naturally of his mature and most characteristic work.) He made no concessions to the delight of all vulgar minds in mere clever craftsmanship. His skill, of course, was enormous, but it was a means, not an end. The texture of his paint is now luminous, now opaque, now rich or tender or craggy, according to the emotion with which he charges it in this passage or that.

But this drama of changing textures, like that of Shakespeare's verse, is subservient to a particular quality that is essentially Rembrandtesque—the drama of light and darkness, the tremendous chiaroscuro through which he manifested his vision, whatever the subject. This was not, of course, his invention. Those who have romanticized the personality of Rembrandt as the eccentric, uneducated, unaccountable 'genius'—in the other, the popular sense—have ignored his obvious scholarship and his debt to Italy. It is true that he never went there, but that does not mean that he did not know and appreciate and even copy Italian work, either from originals in Dutch collections or from engravings. In the

SELF-PORTRAIT. 1658. Canvas. 129×101 cm. New York. Courtesy of the Frick
Collection.

inventory of his own collection we find works attributed to Giorgione, Palma Vecchio, Michelangelo, Bassano the Elder, Raphael and others. His works show the influence of Tintoretto, Ribera and Caravaggio and such of their Northern followers as the Dutch Honthorst and the German Elsheimer.

These are conspicuous for their use of chiaroscuro but it was not only this he learnt from them and from others, but the whole character of Baroque design—the free dramatic movement in space. It does not destroy Rembrandt's originality to recognize this: it merely turns him from an impossible legend into a credible person. His originality, then, does not consist in the sudden invention of a method out of the blue, but in the development of the most vital existing method and its fusion with his own vision so that they became consubstantial. His method *is* his vision: his vision *is* his method. It is then quite arbitrary to consider them apart. It is not that Rembrandt threw a beam of light on to a face or part of a face, on to folded hands or a golden helmet, so that they emerge from shadows of an infinite space in which forms loom here and there in mystery. It is not that. The light *is* the face and the shadow *is* the mystery and the reality revealed exists only in the poetry of their interplay, there and nowhere else.

Rembrandt's production was enormous. Over six hundred authentic paintings, over two hundred etchings and nearly two thousand drawings have survived. In choosing the examples for the proportionately very small selection here, I have concentrated on his two major subjects, the portrait and Biblical events.

He was conditioned by those Dutch circumstances I have mentioned in that he painted many commissioned portraits; but his prosperous sitters emerge not so much like those by his contemporaries as like his own beggars, Rabbis and old women—that most famous parade of unknowns. For Rembrandt gradually lost favour and commissions, and gained freedom to choose his sitters. We must often label a work Portrait of an Unknown Man, but it is, in fact, Portrait of Known Man. Man, indeed, is always Rembrandt's theme and never only a particular sitter. That is why, in his long series of 'portraits' of himself, his mother and father and brother, his wife Saskia and his servant-mistress Hendrickje Stoffels, we find them all so elusive. All these were handy models, himself the handiest, and therefore there survive over sixty accepted self-portraits. They were but particular starting points for what in the end are general statements. The particular homely miller, Harmensz van Rijn, his father, had little to do with the creation called *Rembrandt's Father as an Officer* (Plate 3). It is almost certainly the same model who sat for the *Old Man Asleep* (Plate 1) but his individuality is quite lost in the two new individualities which Rembrandt has created. And if, for example, as is generally believed, his brother sat for *The Man in the Golden Helmet* (Plate 17), what of the everyday shoemaker and miller, Adriaen, is left in this revelation of an iron and sombre soldier? Or consider the amazing series of his self-portraits. In the first group, between about 1629 and 1633, he generally idealized himself, dressing himself up for a great variety of parts. In the earliest I reproduce (Plate 8) he appears as a soldier, but for all the dashing get-up, the helmet, the plume and the careful moustache, what impresses us most is the passionate curiosity with which he peers at his model, which is his multifarious self, that man with the searching, reflective, sad eyes. But he is also the man whom he painted in the same year with his young wife (Plate 9) in the full flush of his first success and gay irresponsible extravagance. The picture invites us into that intimacy. As we enter the room, Rembrandt turns to us, laughing, and raises

7

his glass; and the young Saskia on his knees turns also, a little embarrassed. In the following years he finds himself matured, grown heavy, stately and of immense authority (Frontispiece). Gradually he gives up the fancy dress. His eyes grow sadder and their searching less excitedly eager, more prolonged, reflective and pitying in their gaze. He does not trouble to appear good-looking, and sometimes even emphasizes his clumsy features. Later still, he seems afraid of what he will find in himself and the world. He has achieved the humility of wisdom (Plate 25). The panache is quite gone. And lastly, in the wonderful portrait at Cologne (Plate 26), perhaps his last, he laughs again. But it is a sardonic, quizzical laugh and full of a knowledge which he had not acquired when he laughed with Saskia.

But which of these and all the others is the true Rembrandt? Not one of them, of course: not one, but all. Rembrandt escapes us as Shakespeare does. He, as an individual, is lost in his total creation, which is also where he is found.

It is, for example, the contemplative and studious Rembrandt that we find in a series where he depicts lonely old men and women with books (Plates 6 and 20). He was not himself a reader. They are symbols of his studies in the anatomy of the human soul. We find the romantic Rembrandt, who loved dressing-up and escaping his stolid Amsterdam world, in a whole series of exotic or dressed-up personalities (Plates 7, 10, 11 and 12) for whom his wife or some poor neighbour may have sat—a series that culminates in the astounding *Polish Rider* (Plate 22), which must surely be one of the most completely romantic paintings ever made. And we find the centre of Rembrandt, stripped, neglected, alone and careless of all but the contemplation of sorrow, in the long series of tragic portraits such as those reproduced in Plates 19 and 23.

8

Rembrandt painted remarkably few of the group-portraits which were so popular in Holland, but three of them are among his most celebrated works, although the critic will probably not put them among his profoundest. In *The Anatomy Lesson* (Plate 5) he avoided the boredom of the posed group by dramatizing. The figures are portraits but the picture is genre: it has an existence of its own apart from them. It is not Tulp or his students that interest us because, but for the picture, we should never have heard of them. In the *Parade of the Civic Guard* (Plate 14) Rembrandt's impatience with the group portrait became only too manifest. It is not surprising that the sitters were angry and that it was almost his last such commission; for he turned these men, who had paid to be seen for themselves, into models for a wholly imaginative creation in which some of them are hardly seen at all and a woman is outrageously introduced and conspicuously lit. Here he did not solve the problem of the group portrait but ignored it. And yet, in his last and finest group-portrait (Plate 27), he solved it perfectly. Each man is an individual revealed with his maturest insight and all are grouped into a vital unified design. But all cleverness has disappeared. We are no longer impressed by the ingeniousness of the solution as in the *Anatomy*, but by its apparent inevitability.

Rembrandt explored almost every subject for his art. In this urgent curiosity and experimentation, he was very unlike his countrymen, who generally specialized and kept rigidly to their 'lines', as landscape or seascape, portrait or genre painters. Five Plates, set here between the portraits and Biblical subjects, represent these explorations of Rembrandt's in almost the exact numerical proportion of the paintings. But, of course, they do not correspond to the artistic importance of these 'side-lines'; and in landscape particularly we must take acount of the much higher proportion in his drawings and etchings to appreciate the scope of his response to nature. Altogether they establish him as the greatest of Dutch landscape painters and one of the greatest in Europe. He only painted four still-lifes and they are unimportant except for the *Slaughtered Ox* (Plate 30). The astonishing thing about that picture is its grandeur, that somehow this image of a flayed animal carcase is noble, where so many intended images of God or the Hero are ignoble.

But Rembrandt did not achieve nobility in mythological subjects where it might have been more naturally expected. *Diana Bathing* (Plate 31) is a sensuous and even repellent work. *The Rape of Ganymede* (Plate 32) is frankly comic, although we cannot be sure that Rembrandt meant it to be. His imagination worked with such intensity and so exclusively in its own way, that he may not have appreciated that what came out, in this case, was not a revealing realism but a rude joke at the expense of a poetry he did not understand. In both cases he revealed that element of coarseness which he shared with so many of his contemporaries. It is typical of that element that he should paint the cup-bearer of the gods in the spirit in which they painted the tavern pot-boy; but it was also typical of what was purely himself that he should tackle that theme and not the pot-boy.

But Rembrandt's borrowings from classic mythology or classic history (See Plate 33) are rare. Only one book persistently served his imagination—the Bible. He read it as a record of events in human lives, the matter that was always his chief study. But he was a Christian and, therefore, he also read it as the one source which could give meaning to these events, which for him was a spiritual pattern made of the light that shone in the darkness. We cannot understand Rembrandt if we fail to recognize that he was a deeply religious man; but also we cannot understand him if we expect his work to have the austere grandeurs or pure and radiant symbols which we are accustomed rightly to associate with religious art at its greatest; for Rembrandt was a Protestant Dutchman. Protestants and Dutchmen have produced very little visual religious art of any value. Rembrandt is almost unique. But the quality of his religious art is none the less conditioned by his being Protestant and Dutch. He approached religion through man, above all through the suffering of man. He saw God only in the Man of Sorrows, the frail and outcast *Christ at the Column* (Plate 43) who triumphs only in patience.

But he did not penetrate to his discovery until he had himself suffered. Early works like *The Tribute Money* (Plate 34) are dramatically and scenically effective in a theatrical way. They belong almost to the realm of his 'dressing-up'. But by the time of *The Descent from the Cross* (Plate 35), five years later, he has already outgrown that inappropriate quality. But he has still seen no further than death in this historic event. He can still, as in the *Blinding of Samson* (Plate 36), strive for merciless realism or be content to show *The Holy Family* (Plate 37) as holy only in its tender intimacy. That realism and that holiness are also present in the Plate which faces it here—*The Adoration of the Shepherds*. He has painted the event as it might really have happened in time. The shepherds are indeed shepherds, the stable a stable. Everything is poor and simple. It is a dark night in the stable, lit with common lanterns as he must have seen it when the carter visits his horses on a winter night. But— and this is the tremendous departure from Dutchness, the escape from the event in time to the event in eternity—this stable is also lit with the mystical brightness of the Child. That was the light which he found in the darkness and which he comprehended.

Such overt visitings of the supernatural are comparatively rare in his work—here only in the *St Matthew*, *The Circumcision* and the *Christ at Emmaus* (Plates 44, 45 and 48)—but if the other works of his last twenty years or so are considered by this light, then we understand the significance of his chiaroscuro in them all, which is the poetry of Rembrandt and the symbol of his explanation.

Once this was established as master in his imagination, he discarded all finery and pomp and theatricality. In this light the extreme simplicity of the late works can hold all he charges them with. His final poetry transcends rhetoric as his final love transcends pity and asserts the pattern.

Biographical Notes

1606.　15 July. Rembrandt Harmenszoon van Rijn born in the Weddesteeg, Leyden. His father was a miller; his mother a baker's daughter.

Educated at Latin School, and matriculated at University in 1620, but did not pursue his studies.

1620–24.　Art training under Jacob van Swanenburgh in Leyden and Pieter Lastman in Amsterdam.

1632.　Settled in Amsterdam.

1634.　Married a rich orphan, Saskia van Uylenburgh.

1639.　Bought a house in the St Anthonie-Breestraat, for which he was unable to pay.

1641.　22 September. His son, Titus, baptized.

1642.　14 July. Death of Saskia. Her will gave Rembrandt the use of her fortune until Titus came of age, provided he did not marry.

c. 1645.　Hendrickje Stoffels took service with Rembrandt.

1654.　Birth of Cornelia, Hendrickje's daughter by Rembrandt.

1656.　Rembrandt went bankrupt and inventory taken of his goods (25 July).

1657.　First sale of Rembrandt's property.

1658.　Sale of house and remaining property.

1660.　Rembrandt moved to the Rozengracht and became employee of an art-dealing business which Titus and Hendrickje had set up in 1658.

1661–22.　Possible visit to England, where he was reported (in 1713) to have lived at Hull. This tradition is not usually accepted as possible in view of the work he did in Holland at this time.

1662.　Death of Hendrickje.

1668.　Death of Titus.

1669.　Birth of Titus's posthumous daughter, Titia. Her mother was Magdalena van Loon, whom Titus had married in the year of his death.

4 October. Death of Rembrandt. He was buried in the Westerkerk.

Notes to the Illustrations

All pictures are dated except those where a *circa* or query is indicated.
All paintings are in oil unless otherwise stated.

5. Tulp (1593–1674) was a celebrated anatomist and *praelector anatomiae* at Amsterdam. He is lecturing to seven masters of the Surgeons Guild, whose names are on the paper held by one of them. Until 1828 the picture hung in the Anatomy Theatre of the Guild for which it was painted. It was then bought by William I of the Netherlands.

14. This work has for long been incorrectly called *The Night Watch*. The scene is, in fact, in sunlight. The names of seventeen of the musketeers are written on a shield in the background. The picture originally hung in the Great Hall of the Musketeers Guild. A copy made by Gerrit Lundens in 1660 is in the London National Gallery. It contains two more figures on the left. It is generally believed that this is because a cut of about 20 inches was made in the original; but some experts maintain that these figures are an addition by the copyist.

15. There is no proof that the model for this and many other works of the period is Hendrickje, but it is a reasonable presumption, since she lived with him as maid and mistress from *c*. 1645.

16. The identification is based on an etched portrait of 1651.

17. The sitter for this and other works is commonly identified as Rembrandt's brother, Adriaen; but he appears in one work dated two years after Adriaen's death in 1652.

18. It is generally agreed that this picture represents a subject from classical history or mythology but there is no agreement on its identity or even sex. Mars, Alexander the Great, Apollo, Achilles and Athena have been suggested.

22. When this was exhibited in London in 1910, Sickert wrote: 'London! Like the evening star, you bring me everything. From the other end of nowhere Rembrandt's son rides for a few weeks through the West End, on the white horse, debonair, to an early death, one of the perfect masterpieces of the world.' (Reprinted in *A Free House* ed. by Sir Osbert Sitwell, 1947.)

24. Trip was a Dortrecht merchant. He was also painted by Cuyp and Nicholaes Maes.

14

33. Also called *The Conspiracy of the Batavians*. The incident illustrated is in Tacitus XIII–XV and LXI. Civilis is summoning his companions to swear fealty against the Romans. This is the central portion of a vast composition, estimated to be about six times as large, commissioned for the Town Hall of Amsterdam and set up in 1661. Rembrandt withdrew it for alterations and it was never replaced. It turned up in Sweden between 1785 and 1791, but how it got there remains a mystery. There are four drawings for the complete composition in Munich, one of which is reproduced in the Phaidon edition of the drawings (Plate 279). See Bibliographical Note.

44. The angel is painted from Rembrandt's son, Titus. See Plate 21.

1. OLD MAN ASLEEP AT THE HEARTH. 1629. Panel. 52×41 cm. Turin, Museum.
(Photo: Mansell.)

2. REMBRANDT'S MOTHER. *c.* 1630–1632. Panel. 50×35 cm. Windsor Castle.
By gracious permission of H.M. the Queen.

3. REMBRANDT'S FATHER AS AN OFFICER. *c.* 1630. Panel. 65×51 cm. Sir Brian Mountain, Bt. (Photo: Mansell.)

4. REMBRANDT'S SISTER. 1632. Panel. 55×48 cm. Milan Brera. (Photo: Mansell.)

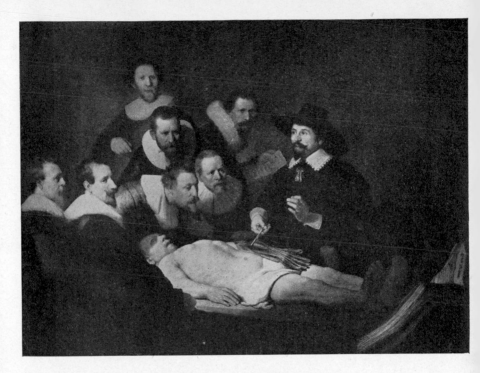

5. THE ANATOMY LESSON OF PROFESSOR NICOLAES TULP. 1632. Canvas. 162·5 × 216·5 cm. The Hague, Mauritshuis.

6. A SCHOLAR SEATED IN AN INTERIOR WITH WINDING STAIR. 1633. Panel. 29 × 33 cm.
Paris, Louvre. (Photo : Mansell.)

7. PORTRAIT OF A DISTINGUISHED ORIENTAL (or THE NOBLE SLAV). 1632. Canvas.
150×121 cm. New York. Courtesy of the Metropolitan Museum of Art.

8. SELF-PORTRAIT WITH HELMET. 1634. Panel. 76×64 cm. Cassel, Museum.

9. SELF-PORTRAIT WITH SASKIA. *c.* 1634. Canvas. 161 × 131 cm. Dresden, Museum.

10. SASKIA. *c.* 1634. Panel. 98×77 cm. Cassel, Museum.

11. AN ORIENTAL IN A WHITE TURBAN. 1635. Panel. 105 × 80 cm. Devonshire Collection, Chatsworth. Reproduced by permission of the Trustees of the Chatsworth Settlement.

12. SASKIA AS FLORA. 1635. Panel. 121·5 × 96·5 cm. London, National Gallery.
Reproduced by courtesy of the Trustees.

13. ALLOTTE ADRIAENS. 1639. Panel. 65 × 56 cm. Sir Francis Cook, Bt., and Trustees of the Cook Collection. (Photo: Mansell.)

14. PARADE OF THE CIVIC GUARD ('THE NIGHT WATCH'). 1642. Canvas. 387×502 cm.
Amsterdam, Rijksmuseum.

15. HENDRICKJE STOFFELS IN BED. *c.* 1649. Canvas. 81 × 67 cm. Edinburgh, National Gallery of Scotland.

16. THE ART DEALER, CLEMENT DE JONGHE. ? *c.* 1651. Canvas. 92·5 × 73·5 cm. Lord Faringdon.

17. THE MAN IN THE GOLDEN HELMET. *c.* 1650. Canvas. 67 × 51·5 cm.
Berlin, State Museum.

18. A MAN IN ARMOUR. 1655. Canvas. 136 × 102·5 cm. Glasgow, Art Gallery.

19. OLD MAN WITH RED FUR CAP. *c.* 1650–1655. Canvas. 51 × 37 cm. Berlin, State Museum. (Photo: Mansell.)

20. AN OLD WOMAN READING. 1655. Canvas. 80×66 cm. Duke of Buccleuch.

21. REMBRANDT'S SON, TITUS. 1655. Canvas. 77×63 cm. Rotterdam, Museum Boymans.

22. THE POLISH RIDER. *c.* 1656. Canvas. 115 × 133·5 cm. New York. Courtesy of the Frick Collection.

23. PORTRAIT OF A RABBI. ?1657. Canvas. 75·5×65·5 cm. London, National Gallery.
Reproduced by courtesy of the Trustees.

24. JACOBSZ TRIP. *c.* 1660. Canvas. 128×96 cm. London, National Gallery.
Reproduced by courtesy of the Trustees.

25. SELF-PORTRAIT AT THE EASEL. 1660. Canvas. 111×85 cm. Paris, Louvre.
(Photo: Mansell.)

26. SELF-PORTRAIT. *c.* 1665. Canvas. 82×63 cm. Cologne, Art Gallery.

27. THE BOARD OF THE CLOTHMAKERS GUILD, AMSTERDAM ('THE SYNDICS'). 1662.
Canvas. 185×274 cm. Amsterdam, Rijksmuseum.

28. A YOUNG WOMAN. 1666. Canvas. 68·5 × 59 cm. London, National Gallery. Reproduced by courtesy of the Trustees.

29. LANDSCAPE WITH STONE BRIDGE AND BOATMEN PUNTING. *c.* 1638. Panel. 29·5 ×
42·5 cm. Amsterdam, Rijksmuseum.

30. THE SLAUGHTERED OX. 1655. Panel. 94×67 cm. Paris, Louvre.
(Photo: Mansell.)

31. DIANA BATHING WITH SCENES FROM THE STORIES OF ACTAEON AND CALLISTO.
1635. Canvas. 72×95 cm. Anholt, Prince Salm-Salm. (Photo: Mansell.)

32. THE RAPE OF GANYMEDE. 1635. Canvas. 171·5 × 130 cm. Dresden, Museum.

33. THE CONSPIRACY OF JULIUS CIVILIS. ?1661. Canvas. 196×309 cm. Stockholm,
National Museum.

34. THE TRIBUTE MONEY. 1629. Panel. 41×33 cm. Sir Alfred Beit, Bt.

35. THE DESCENT FROM THE CROSS. 1634. Canvas. 158 × 117 cm. Leningrad, Hermitage. (Photo: Mansell.)

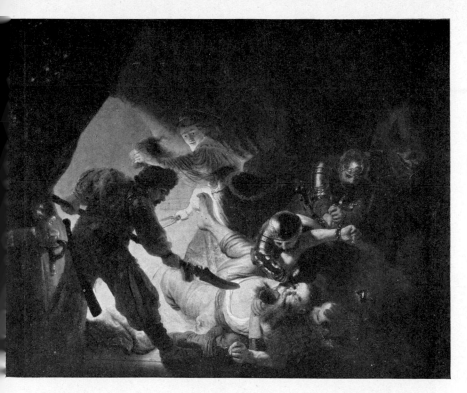

36. THE BLINDING OF SAMSON. 1636. Canvas. 238×287 cm. Frankfort-on-Main, Städel Institute.

37. THE HOLY FAMILY. 1640. Panel. 41 × 34 cm. Paris, Louvre. (Photo: Mansell.)

38. THE ADORATION OF THE SHEPHERDS. 1646. Canvas. 63×55·5 cm. London
National Gallery. Reproduced by courtesy of the Trustees.

39. CHRIST AT EMMAUS. 1648. Canvas. 87·5 × 111 cm. Copenhagen, The Royal Museum of Fine Arts.

40. TOBIT AND HIS WIFE. 1650. Panel. 41·2 × 53·8 cm. Formerly Cook Collection, Richmond. (Photo: Mansell.)

41. CHRIST AND THE WOMAN OF SAMARIA. 1655. Panel. 66·5×39 cm. Berlin State. Museum.

42. JACOB BLESSING HIS GRANDCHILDREN. 1656. Canvas. 174×209 cm. Cassel, Museum.

43. CHRIST AT THE COLUMN. *c.* 1656. Panel. 33×28 cm. Cologne, Museum.

44. ST MATTHEW BEING DICTATED TO BY AN ANGEL. 1661. Canvas. 96×81 cm. Paris, Louvre.

45. THE CIRCUMCISION. 1661. Canvas. 56·5 × 75 cm. National Gallery of Art, Washington, D.C. Widener Collection.

46. RETURN OF THE PRODIGAL SON. *c.* 1668. Canvas. 262 × 205 cm. Leningrad, Hermitage.

47. THE THREE CROSSES. 1653. Etching. (Photo: Mansell.)

48. CHRIST AT EMMAUS. Pen and bistre wash. *c.* 20×18 cm. Formerly Collection of Charles Shannon, R.A.

Bibliographical Notes

Bode, Wilhelm. *The Complete Works of Rembrandt.* 8 vols. Paris, 1896–1906.
de Groot, C. Hofstede. *A Catalogue Raisonné of the Works of the Most Eminent Dutch Painters of the Seventeenth Century,* Vol. VI, sect. xxii. London, 1916.
Bredius, A. *The Paintings of Rembrandt.* Phaidon Press, 1937.
Benesch, O. *Rembrandt, Werk und Forschung.* Vienna, 1935.

These are the standard authorities. Bredius will be found the most generally useful book: it reproduces all paintings accepted by the author. Among recent publications, giving larger but only selected reproductions, I can recommend:

Borenius, T. *Rembrandt. Selected Paintings.* Phaidon Press, 1942 which contains translations of the earliest lives of Rembrandt by Joachim von Sandrart (1675), Filippo Baldinucci (1686) and Arnold Houbraken (1718).
Bodkin, T. *Rembrandt. Paintings.* Apollo ed. London, 1948. Illustrations selected by Professor W. Martin, formerly Director of the Royal Gallery, The Hague.

Writings on Rembrandt are very voluminous and I must recommend the student for full information to the systematic bibliography in the appendix to Dr Benesch's book mentioned above. Another source of information is:

Hall, H. van. *Repertorium voor de Geschiedenis der Nederlandsche Schilderen Graveer Kunst.* The Hague, 1935.

The present volume, being chiefly concerned with Rembrandt's paintings, should be supplemented with:

Benesch, O. *Rembrandt. Selected Drawings.* Phaidon Press, 1947.

This contains 292 plates and is accompanied by an introduction and catalogue raisonné of them in a separate volume. (English text.)